The
Shabbat Book

The Shabbat Book

WRITTEN BY
Joyce Klein

RESEARCH
Jonathan Gillis

EDITORS
Dr. Seymour Epstein
Linda Pardes
Jonathan Lubell

MODEL DESIGN
Dick Codor

CLAY MODELS
Inbal Beter

SETS
Hedda Harari

PHOTOGRAPHY
Shuki Cook Studios

BOOK DESIGN
Utopia Design,
Gali Freedman

PRINTED & BOUND BY
Keterpress Enterprises

The original inspiration for the Shabbat Book,
also published in a Russian edition, came from the
American Jewish Joint Distribution Committee.

Published by Scopus Films
P.O.B. 902, Mevasseret Ziyyon 90805, Israel
©1994 Copyright Scopus Films Ltd.
All rights reserved. ISBN 965-222-529-0

The
Shabbat Book

SCOPUS

There are two important differences between the Jewish calendar and those of the general communities. We name our weeks, not our days; the Gregorian calendar names the days and not the weeks. The Hebrew week is divided into six numbered days leading to the seventh and only day with a name – *Shabbat*. Each week is named after its *Parashat Hashavua*, that week's Torah portion.

This book is dedicated to the idea that a Jew has the capacity to live in Jewish time – Sunday for the Jew becomes *Yom Rishon*, the first of the days leading to Shabbat. The week itself becomes *Breishit*, the first portion of the Torah, or *Mishpatim*, the eighteenth

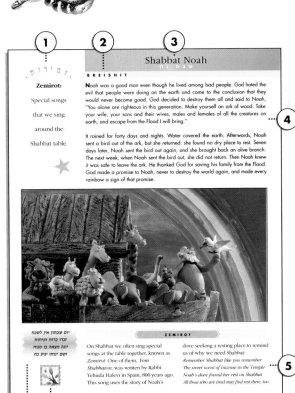

1 A special idea found in the text

2 The transliterated name of the book of the Bible which contains this parasha

3 The transliterated name of the week's parasha with its Hebrew equivalent

4 An overview of highlights from the parasha

5 A Shabbat prayer, custom, thought or tale

6 The page number; the season in which we read this parasha

7 Original Hebrew corresponding to the italicized English translation in the text

portion and so on. **The Shabbat Book,** in both form and content, teaches us that a Jew looks forward to and prepares for Shabbat all week. During the week a Jew carries with him the narrative, ideas, *mitzvot* and emotions of that week's Torah portion. Over the centuries throughout the world, Shabbat in all its glory and the multi-faceted teachings of the Torah have influenced the lives of individual Jews, their families and their communities.

We hope that as children study the content of a Torah portion each week, along with something new about Shabbat, the influence of these two great Jewish institutions, Shabbat and Torah, will be cultivated in a new generation of Jews.

Dr. Seymour Epstein
Director of Jewish Education,
American Jewish Joint Distribution Committee

This is the Jewish people's story of how the world began. It is a description of how God created a whole world from nothing: light and darkness, the sky, the earth, the oceans and seas, the plants that grow, the sun, moon and stars, the creatures that swim, fly, creep and walk and, finally, human beings.

Creation is divided into seven parts. They are called "days" – but it's hard to know what a day was before there was a sun! It could have lasted hours or years, because time did not yet exist. The first six "days" are divisions of creation. The seventh is Shabbat, the day of rest, when creation was completed. Along with a world, God gave humanity a gift: the day God rested from creation became our day of rest – Shabbat.

2

Rabbi Abraham Joshua Heschel did a lot of thinking about Shabbat. He called Shabbat "a palace in time." On Shabbat, he said, we are told to be free of things. We are given a day of harmony and peace with nature, between people and within ourselves. On Shabbat we are asked not to change the world, but to enjoy it as it is.

The first thing God called "holy" was not a place or a thing – it was time, the seventh day, Shabbat.

KIDDUSH

Part 1: There are many customs and rituals for celebrating Shabbat. One of them is *Kiddush:* a ritual of wine. The family gathers around the dinner table. Someone lifts a full glass of wine, as a symbol of celebration, and chants the Kiddush prayer. The first half of that prayer comes from this week's parasha, *Breishit.*

The heavens and the earth and all they contained were finished. On the seventh day, God finished the work of creation, and rested. God blessed the day and made it holy, because it was a day of rest.

When we say Kiddush, we are like witnesses to the creation of the world. We thank God for our world, and for Shabbat. Because we do this every week, we never forget how grateful we are for what we have, and we make each Shabbat holy.

The second half of the Kiddush comes from *Shabbat Lech Lecha.*

וַיְכֻלּוּ הַשָּׁמַיִם וְהָאָרֶץ

וְכָל צְבָאָם. וַיְכַל

אֱלֹהִים בַּיּוֹם הַשְּׁבִיעִי

מְלַאכְתּוֹ אֲשֶׁר עָשָׂה,

וַיִּשְׁבֹּת בַּיּוֹם הַשְּׁבִיעִי מִכָּל־

מְלַאכְתּוֹ אֲשֶׁר עָשָׂה.

וַיְבָרֶךְ אֱלֹהִים אֶת יוֹם

הַשְּׁבִיעִי וַיְקַדֵּשׁ

אֹתוֹ, כִּי בוֹ שָׁבַת מִכָּל־

מְלַאכְתּוֹ אֲשֶׁר בָּרָא

אֱלֹהִים לַעֲשׂוֹת.

3

Shabbat Noah
שַׁבָּת נֹחַ

Zemirot:

Special songs

that we sing

around the

Shabbat table.

Noah was a good man even though he lived among bad people. God hated the evil that people were doing on the earth and came to the conclusion that they would never become good. God decided to destroy them all and said to Noah, "You alone are righteous in this generation. Make yourself an ark of wood. Take your wife, your sons and their wives, males and females of all the creatures on earth, and escape from the Flood I will bring."

It rained for forty days and nights. Water covered the earth. Afterwards, Noah sent a bird out of the ark, but she returned: she found no dry place to rest. Seven days later, Noah sent the bird out again, and she brought back an olive branch. The next week, when Noah sent the bird out, she did not return. Then Noah knew it was safe to leave the ark. He thanked God for saving his family from the Flood. God made a promise to Noah, never to destroy the world again, and made every rainbow a sign of that promise.

יוֹם שַׁבָּתוֹן אֵין לִשְׁכּוֹחַ
זִכְרוֹ כְּרֵיחַ הַנִּיחוֹחַ
יוֹנָה מָצְאָה בוֹ מָנוֹחַ
וְשָׁם יָנוּחוּ יְגִיעֵי כֹחַ

ZEMIROT

On Shabbat we often sing special songs at the table together, known as *Zemirot*. One of them, *Yom Shabbaton*, was written by Rabbi Yehuda Halevi in Spain, 800 years ago. This song uses the story of Noah's dove seeking a resting place to remind us of why we need Shabbat:

Remember Shabbat like you remember
The sweet scent of incense in the Temple
Noah's dove found her rest on Shabbat
All those who are tired may find rest there, too

Shabbat Lech Lecha
שַׁבַּת לֶךְ לְךָ

B R E I S H I T

Avraham was a man chosen by God. God said to Avraham, "Get up and leave the land where you were born and your parents lived, and go to a place I will show you." So, Avraham and Sarah, his wife, traveled from Haran to Canaan (which is Israel today). Once they got to Canaan, God made a promise: that Avraham would be the father of a great nation in this land, a nation that would be blessed by all the nations of the world, a nation with a special bond to God forevermore.

K I D D U S H

Part 2: The second half of the Friday night Kiddush talks about God's promise to Avraham – and to all the members of the Jewish people. First, however, comes the blessing we say over the wine.

Blessed are You, God,
Who created the fruit of the vine
Blessed are You, God,
who made us holy with commandments,
Who wanted us,
Who gave us the holy Shabbat with love,
as a reminder of the story of creation.

You chose us and made us holy
from all other nations
Blessed are You, God,
Who makes Shabbat holy.

This is our covenant, our agreement, with God: God chooses us, commands us, and gives us Shabbat. We accept God's commandments and agree to be chosen. The symbol of this covenant is Shabbat, and every week we remind ourselves, and God, that we remember it.

בָּרוּךְ אַתָּה יְיָ

אֱלֹהֵינוּ מֶלֶךְ הָעוֹלָם

בּוֹרֵא פְּרִי הַגָּפֶן

בָּרוּךְ אַתָּה יְיָ

אֱלֹהֵינוּ מֶלֶךְ הָעוֹלָם

אֲשֶׁר קִדְּשָׁנוּ

בְּמִצְוֹתָיו וְרָצָה בָנוּ

וְשַׁבַּת קָדְשׁוֹ

בְּאַהֲבָה וּבְרָצוֹן הִנְחִילָנוּ

זִכָּרוֹן לְמַעֲשֵׂה בְרֵאשִׁית...

כִּי בָנוּ בָחַרְתָּ וְאוֹתָנוּ

קִדַּשְׁתָּ מִכָּל הָעַמִּים...

בָּרוּךְ אַתָּה יְיָ

מְקַדֵּשׁ הַשַּׁבָּת

5

BREISHIT

One day, three strangers appeared near Avraham's tent. Avraham ran after them and offered them hospitality. "Wash the dust from your feet and rest in my shade," he said. Avraham and Sarah prepared food and served the strangers. One of them said to Avraham, "I will return in one year, and Sarah then will have a son." Sarah, who was listening in the tent, laughed at the thought that she could have a child, because she was too old. But a year later, a son was born to Sarah and Avraham, and they called him Yitzchak, from the Hebrew word "to laugh."

מדרש.

Midrash:

A story

of the Rabbis

that explains

and adds

to the Torah.

SHABBAT GUESTS

One of the best ways of celebrating Shabbat is to invite guests for one of the Shabbat meals, or just for a visit on Shabbat afternoon, when everyone has time to spend with friends. Avraham was famous for welcoming all guests, even strangers, into his tent. This week's parasha gives us a sample of his graciousness. It is a *mitzvah,* a commandment and good deed, to invite guests to our homes. This is an especially enjoyable mitzvah!

Some of the Rabbis from long ago thought of Shabbat itself as a guest we welcome into our homes every week, with songs and candles and good food to eat. They called Shabbat a queen, *Shabbat Hamalka,* and composed special songs and prayers in her honor.

Shabbat Hayei Sarah
שבת חיי שרה

Sarah died, and Avraham mourned her. He bought the cave of Machpela as a burial place. Then Avraham called his servant, Eliezer, and said, "Go to the land of my birth and find a wife for my son, Yitzchak." On the journey, Eliezer asked God to help him find the right woman. He created a plan: he would ask the young women of the place for water to drink. Any of them who was kind enough to offer water to his camels as well would be the right sort of wife for Yitzchak.

When Eliezer met Rivka, who turned out to be Avraham's great-niece, she did exactly that, and even more. Rivka and her family agreed to the match, and Eliezer brought her back to Canaan. Yitzchak married Rivka, and his love for her comforted him after his mother's death. Avraham died and was buried near Sarah.

CANDLE LIGHTING

There is a midrash which says that Sarah started the custom of lighting candles on Shabbat. When she died, no one lit Shabbat candles in Avraham's tent – until Rivka married Yitzchak. Rivka brought back the Shabbat lights to Avraham and Yitzchak.

From then until today, Shabbat has begun just before sunset on Friday night with the lighting of the Shabbat candles. Most people light two candles, although some light a candle for every member of the family. Usually, it is the woman who does the lighting, in the tradition of Sarah and Rivka. A *bracha*, a blessing, is said when the candles are lit:

Blessed are You, God,
Who has made us holy
and commanded us
to light the Shabbat candles

Just as the candles must have brightened Avraham's tent, we are brightened by the light of Shabbat.

בָּרוּךְ אַתָּה יְיָ

אֱלֹהֵינוּ מֶלֶךְ הָעוֹלָם

אֲשֶׁר קִדְּשָׁנוּ

בְּמִצְוֹתָיו

וְצִוָּנוּ לְהַדְלִיק נֵר

שֶׁל שַׁבָּת

7

Shabbat Toldot
שבת תולדות

Parasha:

Parasha:

Each Shabbat of the year is known by the name of the section of the Torah which belongs to that day. In the synagogue, that section is chanted aloud. In schools and homes, people study that Shabbat's "parasha" all week. That way, we read and study the whole Torah every year.

Rivka gave birth to twins. The firstborn was Esav, an outdoors type. His brother, Ya'akov, was quieter. Yitzchak favored Esav and Rivka favored Ya'akov (parents are like that sometimes). Once, Ya'akov was cooking a lentil stew when Esav came back from hunting. He was starving and wanted some of the stew. Ya'akov said, "First sell me your rights as firstborn." Esav agreed and ate the stew.

Many years later, when Yitzchak grew old and blind, he asked Esav to hunt something special for him before receiving Yitzchak's final blessing. While Esav was out hunting, Rivka convinced Ya'akov to masquerade as Esav, bring his father a meal that he loved and receive the firstborn's blessing. Rivka dressed him in Esav's clothing, put sheep's wool on his arms (because Esav was a hairy man), and gave him food to take to his father. Yitzchak was confused, saying, "The voice is Ya'akov's, but the hands are Esav's." He gave Ya'akov the blessing. Esav returned and learned what had happened. He cried bitterly, but then he became furious, and plotted revenge against his brother, so Rivka sent Ya'akov to visit her family, telling Yitzchak he was going to look for a wife. In this way Ya'akov was protected from his brother.

CHOLENT

Food is an important factor in this week's parasha – as it is on every Jewish occasion. Ya'akov's lentil stew reminds us of a special dish that was invented because of Shabbat. Some Jews call it *cholent* or *shalett,* others call it *hamin.*

It is always a rich stew that cooks all night in the oven, to be ready for lunch on Shabbat. The smell of it cooking makes the whole house smell like Shabbat, and makes everyone hungry enough to sell their firstborn rights!

Shabbat Vayetse
שבת ויצא

Ya'akov left his parents' home and set off for his Uncle Lavan's in Haran. One night on his journey, he had a dream: a ladder stood on the ground with its top in heaven, and angels moved up and down on it. Then God appeared and blessed Ya'akov with the same blessing as God had given Avraham and Yitzchak.

In Haran, Ya'akov fell in love with his cousin, Rachel, and promised to work seven years in order to marry her. But when the time was up, Lavan tricked Ya'akov. He substituted Leah, Rachel's older sister, as the bride! Lavan gave Ya'akov permission to marry Rachel as well (more than one wife at the same time was common then) in exchange for seven more years of work. Ya'akov's family, and his flocks grew and prospered. When it was time for him to take his family back to Canaan, he had eleven sons and a daughter, and was a wealthy man. God's blessing was starting to come true.

KABALAT SHABBAT

When Shabbat begins, we call the first prayer service *Kabalat Shabbat*. This phrase means two different things: "accepting Shabbat" and "greeting Shabbat". We accept all the obligations, rules and rituals of Shabbat – but we also welcome Shabbat, greet it like an important person. That is why Shabbat is referred to both as a queen and as a bride – we accept her obligations, and we greet her with love.

9

Shabbat Vayishlach
שַׁבָּת וַיִּשְׁלַח

On Ya'akov's journey home, he stayed alone one night, and an angel – a messenger of God – met him there. They wrestled until daybreak. Although Ya'akov was hurt, he was also blessed by the angel, who changed his name to *Israel,* which means, "you have struggled with God." Ya'akov and Esav were reunited after twenty years. Rachel, Ya'akov's beloved wife, died on the journey, giving birth to his twelfth son, Binyamin. Ya'akov reached his father's tent in time to spend some years with him before Yitzchak died. The brothers buried their father in the cave of Machpela.

שָׁלוֹם עֲלֵיכֶם

מַלְאֲכֵי הַשָּׁרֵת

מַלְאֲכֵי עֶלְיוֹן

מִמֶּלֶךְ מַלְכֵי הַמְּלָכִים

הַקָּדוֹשׁ בָּרוּךְ הוּא

. . . .

בּוֹאֲכֶם לְשָׁלוֹם...

. . . .

בָּרְכוּנִי לְשָׁלוֹם...

. . . .

צֵאתְכֶם לְשָׁלוֹם...

TWO ANGELS

There is a midrash that says that every Jew is accompanied home on Friday night by two angels: one good and one evil. When they arrive, if the Shabbat candles are lit, the table is set, and the house is clean and ready for Shabbat, the good angel says, "May next Shabbat be just like this one." And the evil angel must answer, "Amen."

But if no candles are lit, the house is dirty and nothing is ready for Shabbat, then the evil angel says, "May next Shabbat be just like this one," and the good angel must answer, "Amen."

There is a song that is sung by the family to begin the Friday night Shabbat meal. In it, the family sings to the two angels in the midrash. They are also greeting Shabbat itself.

Greetings to you, Angels!
May peace enter with you,
Bless me for peace,
Go on your way in peace
God is over us all

10

Shabbat Vayeshev
שבת וישב

Ya'akov's favorite son was Yosef, and Ya'akov gave him a beautiful coat. Yosef knew he was the favorite, and acted like it – which made his brothers very jealous. (Children are like that sometimes.) Once, when all the brothers were far from home, they decided to sell Yosef to some passing traders and tell their father he had been killed by a wild animal. (Well, most children aren't like *that*.)

The traders took Yosef to Egypt where he was a slave for a while. Even as a slave, Yosef tried to live by his father's covenant with God. Partly because of his beliefs, and partly because of a misunderstanding, Yosef was thrown into prison. There, he interpreted dreams for the Pharaoh's chief baker (who was killed) and his chief butler (who was freed). The butler, once free, forgot Yosef, so Yosef remained a prisoner.

CREATING SHABBAT

What is it the angels (or anyone else...) would find that creates the look, the feel, the blessing of Shabbat?

Shabbat candles: at least two candles are lit because the Torah gives two commandments about Shabbat, *Keep the Shabbat* and *Remember the Shabbat*. Actually, candles have only been used for 300 years or so. Before that, Jews used bowls made of clay, silver or copper, hung from the ceiling, with wicks in olive oil, for their Shabbat lights.

A bottle of wine or grape juice, and a Kiddush cup: the Kiddush cup is often made of silver or decorated glass. Since it is the most important cup on the table and will be used for a mitzvah, it should be special.

The house: a house that has been prepared for Shabbat is clean, filled with good smells of the dinner about to be served. The table is set as nicely as possible to honor the Shabbat.

11

Shabbat Miketz
שבת מקץ

BREISHIT

Pharaoh, the ruler of all Egypt, had dreams that no one could understand, of seven skinny cows eating seven fat cows, and other strange things. Then his butler remembered Yosef, who was brought before Pharaoh, where he interpreted the dreams. He also advised Pharaoh on how to handle the famine he predicted from the dreams. Pharaoh was so impressed that he made Yosef his deputy.

When famine came to the region, Egypt did not suffer (because of Yosef). But back in Canaan, the famine was hard, and Ya'akov sent his sons to Egypt to look for food. They didn't recognize their brother, but Yosef recognized *them*. He decided to accuse them of being spies, imprisoned one of them, and arranged for his youngest brother, Binyamin, to be imprisoned next.

LECHAH DODI

לְכָה דוֹדִי לִקְרַאת כַּלָּה

פְּנֵי שַׁבָּת נְקַבְּלָה

. . . .

לִקְרַאת שַׁבָּת לְכוּ וְנֵלְכָה

כִּי הִיא מְקוֹר הַבְּרָכָה

מֵרֹאשׁ מִקֶּדֶם נְסוּכָה

סוֹף מַעֲשֶׂה

בְּמַחֲשָׁבָה תְּחִלָּה

. . . .

בּוֹאִי בְשָׁלוֹם עֲטֶרֶת בַּעְלָהּ

גַּם בְּשִׂמְחָה וּבְצָהֳלָה

תּוֹךְ אֱמוּנֵי עַם סְגֻלָּה

בּוֹאִי כַלָּה, בּוֹאִי כַלָּה

There are prayers that are said on Friday night to welcome the Shabbat. Some families sing the Shabbat prayers at home, around the table. Others go to synagogue and join the whole community in welcoming Shabbat.

The most famous Friday night prayer is a song called *Lechah Dodi*. Long ago, in the sixteenth century, a group of Jews lived in the city of Tsfat, in northern Israel. They were mystics – they tried to find ways to get closer to God. On Friday nights they would dress all in white, and go out into the fields. There, they would watch the sun set, and greet Shabbat as it arrived by singing *Lechah Dodi*, a song their rabbi had written. Today, Jews everywhere sing it to welcome Shabbat. The chorus says:

Come, my beloved friend,
Let us greet the Bride
And welcome Shabbat as she arrives

Lechah Dodi sees Shabbat as a bride all in white, with God as her groom.

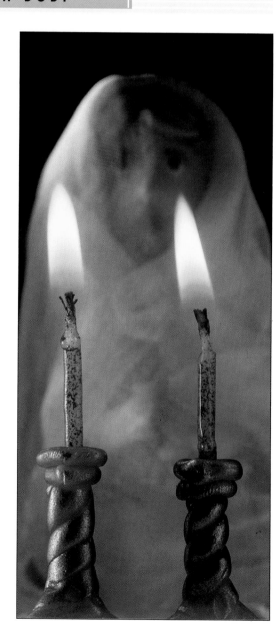

12

Shabbat Vayigash
שבת ויגש

Yehudah, one of Yosef's brothers, spoke to Yosef from the heart, and offered to go to prison in place of Binyamin. Yosef was overcome, and finally said to his brothers, "I am Yosef. Is my father still alive?" After a tearful reunion and forgiveness, Yosef sent his brothers to Canaan to bring Ya'akov back to Egypt. Pharaoh gave them the land of Goshen. Ya'akov, with all of his family and possessions, came down to Egypt and to his long-lost favorite son.

Lechah Dodi has many verses. We will look at two of them:

We will go out to meet Shabbat
Because she is
the source of all blessings
Destined for greatness
from earliest time
The end of creation,
but first in God's thought

Come in peace,
The crown of your groom
In joy and celebration
You are the center
Of the chosen people's faith
Come, Shabbat bride, come!

Lechah Dodi is a love song to Shabbat. It is a celebration of what Shabbat has always meant to the Jewish people.

13

Shabbat Vayehi
שבת ויחי

Ya'akov knew he would not live much longer. He asked his sons to promise that his bones would be buried in Canaan, with those of Avraham and Yitzchak. Ya'akov gave a special blessing to Yosef's sons, Ephraim and Menashe. He put his hands on their heads and blessed them in the name of the God of Avraham, Yitzchak and Ya'akov. He said, "All the people of Israel will say as a blessing: May God make you like Ephraim and Menashe."

Ya'akov blessed all of his children, and then he died. All of Egypt mourned him. Not long afterward Yosef, too, died in the land of Egypt.

BLESSING THE CHILDREN

Shabbat is, above all, a time for the family. In some families, Friday night is the one night of the week that all members of the family have dinner together. There are many customs and rituals that happen at the Shabbat table that are family oriented.

One of these is the blessing of the children by the parents. As we saw throughout the book of *Breishit*, this is a very old custom. Even today, we use both the words and the method that Ya'akov used in this week's parasha to bless our children.

The blessing is said either after lighting the Shabbat candles, or just before Kiddush. Both customs are common. Parents (either mother, or father, or both) put their hands on their children's heads for the blessing.

14

Breishit is a book full of stories about families. There is love, devotion and sacrifice in it – and anger, jealousy, rivalry and revenge. (*All* families are like that sometimes!) At the end of *Breishit,* Ya'akov's family finds itself in Egypt. The next part of the story, as the family becomes a people, begins next week.

For boys: *May God make you like Ephraim and Menashe.*

For girls: *May God make you like Sarah, Rivka, Rachel, and Leah.*

For both: *May God bless you and keep you. May God's light shine upon you. May God's face be turned toward you and give you peace.*

Kisses after the blessings are optional.

לְבָנִים

יְשִׂימְךָ אֱלֹהִים

כְּאֶפְרַיִם וְכִמְנַשֶּׁה

. . . .

לְבָנוֹת

יְשִׂימֵךְ אֱלֹהִים כְּשָׂרָה

רִבְקָה רָחֵל וְלֵאָה

. . . .

לְכֻלָּם

יְבָרֶכְךָ יְיָ וְיִשְׁמְרֶךָ

יָאֵר יְיָ פָּנָיו

אֵלֶיךָ וִיחֻנֶּךָּ

יִשָּׂא יְיָ פָּנָיו אֵלֶיךָ

וְיָשֵׂם לְךָ שָׁלוֹם

15

A new Pharaoh who never knew Yosef came to power in Egypt. He was worried about Ya'akov's family – the Children of Israel – who had grown to a great number. Pharaoh made them all slaves and ordered all newborn males drowned. Then, Moshe was born, and his mother hid him until he was too big to hide anymore. As a last resort, she tucked him into a basket and put it into the River Nile. His sister, Miriam, kept watch to see what became of him; Pharaoh's daughter found him, rescued him, and raised him as her own in the palace. When he grew up, Moshe learned that he, too, was an Israelite.

One day, God spoke to Moshe, and convinced him that, with God's help, he could lead his people out of slavery. Moshe and his brother, Aharon, went to Pharaoh and asked that the Children of Israel be allowed to leave. Pharaoh was so angry that he made the work of the slaves even harder. The people complained bitterly, but God said to Moshe: "You shall soon see what I will do to Pharaoh."

16

Whenever Shabbat is mentioned in the Torah, God or Moshe ususally add: "Remember you were once slaves in the land of Egypt." There is nothing that makes us appreciate Shabbat more than reading a parasha like this one, in which we remember what it was like to be slaves. In Egypt, someone else decided what our life would be like, and what we would do every moment.

Sometimes, our lives today feel like that. We feel like "slaves" to school and schedules or to the decisions of parents or teachers. But on Shabbat, we are free of the daily life we lead, and have the time to remember that we are also human.

Shabbat Va-era
שבת וארא

God said to Moshe: I remember my covenant with Avraham, Yitzchak and Ya'akov. I hear the suffering of the Children of Israel. Tell them: I will free you, I will take you to be My people and I will be your God.

Moshe warned Pharaoh of the plagues God would bring to Egypt if he did not let the people go. Aharon turned the waters of the Nile river into blood; he brought frogs that got into everything; he brought terrible lice, swarms of "wild things" (some people interpret this as insects) that invaded the houses; a strange disease that attacked and killed animals; boils that covered human skin and huge hailstones that destroyed the crops. Each time, Pharaoh said: Stop the plague and you may leave! But when the plague was removed, Pharaoh's heart was hardened, and he changed his mind.

SLAVERY

What does it mean to be a slave? Another side of being a slave is being nameless, just one of a crowd of people whose lives are not their own. On Shabbat, we celebrate being part of a people with a special destiny.

We usually celebrate with our family. Shabbat is the opposite of slavery; that is why we say in the Kiddush that Shabbat reminds us of being freed from slavery in Egypt.

18

Shabbat Bo
שַׁבָּת בֹּא

Three more plagues remained. Moshe brought locusts that ate everything left growing. Then a black night fell on Egypt for three days, so dark, people could not move or see their hands in front of their eyes. Finally, God caused every Egyptian firstborn, animal and child, to die in the middle of the night. Pharaoh sent for Moshe and Aharon and said: Go, all of you! Leave us and go to your God.

That night was the first night of Pesach. The people prepared bread for the journey, but the dough had no time to rise. They baked it anyway, and that was how *matzah* was created. The people left Egypt as quickly as they could. The Children of Israel walked from slavery into freedom.

זֵכֶר
לִיצִיאַת
מִצְרָיִם

FREEDOM

What does it mean to be free? We must have dreamed of freedom when we were slaves in Egypt. On Shabbat, we can give that freedom to others, and maybe that will make us free, too. On Shabbat, we are commanded to give our servants and animals a day of rest. We do not ask them to work for us. We let go of our power over people, animals and things. They are free of us, and we are free of them.

19

Shabbat B'shalach/Shira
שבת בשלח/שירה

SHEMOT

The Children of Israel, hundreds of thousands of them, left Egypt. The Egyptian army followed them – Pharaoh changed his mind again! – but God caused the Sea of Reeds (today called the Red Sea) to split into two standing walls of water, so Israel could escape. When the army tried to follow, the sea returned to its place and drowned them. The people were saved and sang a song of praise and thanks: the *Shira*. Then Miriam sang another song, and the women danced in celebration. So this Shabbat is called *Shabbat Shira*.

Now the people set off through the desert to the land promised them by God. But they had to eat. God provided them with *manna* – a white substance that fell every morning with the dew. The people gathered enough for each day. But on Friday, they gathered a double portion, so they would have enough for Shabbat.

8 Shabbatot:

There are eight special Shabbatot every year. They are always in the same order. Some always fall on the same parasha; others do not.

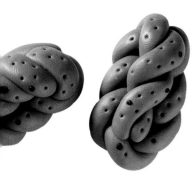

CHALLAH

We remember this week's parasha every week on our Shabbat table. It is the custom to have two loaves of *challah,* a special, sweet bread, on our Shabbat table. They remind us of the double portion of manna God provided for Shabbat in the desert.

SINGING ON SHABBAT

There is a midrash that tells that the Children of Israel forgot how to sing while they were slaves in Egypt. After they crossed the Sea of Reeds, the birds taught them to sing again. Today there is a custom to feed the birds on *Shabbat Shira,* to thank them for teaching us to sing.

Shabbat Yitro
שַׁבַּת יִתְרוֹ

The Children of Israel arrived at Mount Sinai, the Mountain of God. Moshe told them to prepare themselves for three days for the giving of the *Torah*, the book God would give them to guide them as a nation. The day arrived, with thunder and lightning, the sound of the shofar and smoke from the mountain. Through the noise and the fire, they heard God speak to them. They were given ten basic rules, the heart of the Torah. Hearing the voice of God frightened them so much that after the first two commandments, Moshe went up the mountain to receive the rest of the Torah for them.

זָכוֹר אֶת

יוֹם הַשַּׁבָּת

לְקַדְּשׁוֹ

שֵׁשֶׁת יָמִים

תַּעֲבֹד וְעָשִׂיתָ

כָּל מְלַאכְתֶּךָ

וְיוֹם הַשְּׁבִיעִי

שַׁבָּת לַיָי

אֱלֹהֶיךָ

REMEMBERING SHABBAT

The fourth of the Ten Commandments (as the ten basic rules are known) is recited as part of the Kiddush at the second meal of Shabbat – Shabbat lunch:

*Remember the Shabbat
to keep it holy.
Six days you shall work,*
*but the seventh day
is your God's Shabbat.
You shall do no work;
You, your son and daughter,
your male and female slave,
your animals and the stranger
who live among you.*

21

Shabbat Mishpatim
שבת משפטים

The Children of Israel are becoming a nation, and God teaches them the obligations and laws attached to nationhood. In this parasha, it is as if we are listening to some of what God is teaching Moshe on top of Mount Sinai. There are laws against stealing and cheating, about taking care of the poor, about being kind to strangers. Here is one law: If you take your neighbor's garment as a pledge for a loan, you must return it to him before the sun sets – otherwise he will have nothing to cover himself while he sleeps. The laws of the Torah are meant to create a nation of people who care about each other.

LAWS

It may seem strange that we need laws in order to be free, but we do. Laws are much more than a list of "do's" and "don'ts." They create experiences that shape the people who live by them. There are many laws connected to Shabbat. The laws of Shabbat try to create an atmosphere in which the day can be experienced in a special,

unique way. For example, observant Jews do not drive or ride in cars (or buses or trains or planes) on Shabbat. This means that they must live close enough to their synagogue to walk to it. The result is that observant Jews end up living in the same neighborhood and visiting each other on Shabbat. So the rule creates a community.

Shabbat Terumah/Shekalim
שבת תרומה/שקלים

Even though the Children of Israel were traveling in the desert, they needed a special place as a symbol of God's presence among them. God commanded them to build a *Mishkan*, a movable sanctuary that would be set up each time they camped. Many materials were needed to build the Mishkan: gold, silver, copper, wool, linen, wood and precious stones. The people were asked to contribute as they wished, so that the Mishkan could be built.

This Shabbat is also known as *Shabbat Shekalim.* A special reading is added which describes how each person gave half a *shekel*, an ancient coin, so the people could be counted. These donations were used for sacrifices and to keep the Mishkan beautiful.

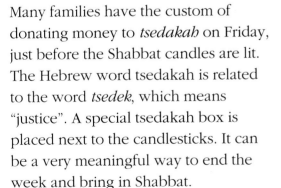

TSEDAKAH

Many families have the custom of donating money to *tsedakah* on Friday, just before the Shabbat candles are lit. The Hebrew word tsedakah is related to the word *tsedek*, which means "justice". A special tsedakah box is placed next to the candlesticks. It can be a very meaningful way to end the week and bring in Shabbat.

As we see in this week's parasha, the idea of donating money for the community is a very ancient Jewish tradition.

. צ ד ק ה .

Tsedakah:

The ancient Jewish

tradition of

donating money

for the community.

23

מ ש כ ן

Mishkan:

A movable

sanctuary

to be set up

each time

the Children

of Israel

camped.

God tells Moshe to have a constant light, a *Ner Tamid*, burning in the Mishkan. It will burn with olive oil given by the people, throughout the generations. Aharon and his descendants are set apart as *Kohanim*, priests, who will serve God and care for the Mishkan. (Today, all synagogues have a Ner Tamid in them, and the descendants of Aharon still know that they are set apart.)

This Shabbat is also known as *Shabbat Zachor*. A special reading is added, the story of Amalek, a tribe that attacked Israel with great cruelty just after they left Egypt. *Shabbat Zachor* falls before Purim, when we read the story of another great enemy of the Jews, Haman. *Shabbat Zachor* reminds us of Amalek's inhumanity in the hope that the Amalek spirit may be erased from the human heart.

NER TAMID

The Midrash teaches that the Ner Tamid was a symbol of Israel as "a light unto the nations" – a nation with something important to teach the world. A.L. Ginsberg, also known as *Achad Ha'am*, "One of the People", was a writer who once said: More than Israel has kept the Shabbat, Shabbat has kept Israel. He believed that the idea of Shabbat was a kind of Ner Tamid for the Jews, that burns throughout generations and reminds us of who we are.

SHEMOT

All this time, Moshe had been up on Mount Sinai, receiving the Torah from God. He came down the mountain carrying two tablets of stone, symbolizing the Torah. When Moshe arrived, he was shocked to find the people worshipping a golden calf that they had persuaded Aharon to make for them out of their own jewelry and gold. Moshe was so angry that he broke the tablets and punished the people. Then he went back up the mountain and received another set of tablets from God.

This Shabbat is also known as *Shabbat Parah,* referring to an unusual ritual of purification using the ashes of a *parah adumah,* a red heifer. We read it with the story of the golden calf, to remind us that there was a need for purification after that terrible sin.

וְשָׁמְרוּ בְּנֵי יִשְׂרָאֵל

אֶת הַשַּׁבָּת

לַעֲשׂוֹת אֶת הַשַּׁבָּת

לְדֹרֹתָם

בְּרִית עוֹלָם

בֵּינִי וּבֵין בְּנֵי יִשְׂרָאֵל

אוֹת הִיא לְעֹלָם

כִּי שֵׁשֶׁת יָמִים

עָשָׂה יְיָ אֶת הַשָּׁמַיִם

וְאֶת הָאָרֶץ

וּבַיּוֹם הַשְּׁבִיעִי

שָׁבַת וַיִּנָּפַשׁ

KIDDUSH

This parasha contains the first paragraph of the Kiddush for Shabbat lunch: *The Children of Israel shall keep Shabbat throughout the generations as a covenant for all time between God and the people. For God made heaven and earth in six days, and on the seventh day God rested and was refreshed in spirit.*

25

Hidur Mitzvah:

The idea

of making our

fulfillment

of God's

Bezalel, from the tribe of Judah, was endowed by God with "a divine spirit of skill, ability and knowledge in every kind of craft." He, along with many other skilled individuals, took the materials from the people and the design God had given and built the Mishkan. When it was completed, Moshe blessed them. From then on the Mishkan became the center of the Israelite camp.

This Shabbat is also known as *Shabbat Hachodesh*, because it falls on the first Shabbat of the *chodesh*, the month, of Nissan. The special reading is about Nissan, when the people left Egypt.

commandments

beautiful.

HIDUR MITZVAH

Bezalel was selected to build the Mishkan because he would make it beautiful. The idea of making our fulfillment of God's commandments beautiful is called *Hidur Mitzvah*. Although we are given many commandments about Shabbat, it is Hidur Mitzvah that causes us to want our houses to be beautiful, to use special Kiddush cups, to set aside the best food we can afford for Shabbat. It honors God and Shabbat, and helps us appreciate our celebration.

Shabbat Hachodesh
שבת החודש

SHEMOT

We read two parshiot this Shabbat for a very practical reason: when it is not a leap year, there are not enough Shabbatot to read each parasha on its own, so some are put together.

YOSEF MOKIR SHABBAT

There was once a very poor man called Yosef. The people of the town used to call him *Yosef Mokir Shabbat,* which means "Yosef who treasures Shabbat," because whatever he had and whatever he earned, however little, he would spend on something special for Shabbat. The merchants in the marketplace knew that even as late as Friday afternoon, they could expect Yosef to wander into the market, looking for that special delicacy which he couldn't afford, but which he'd buy anyway.

Now, in a nearby town lived a rich merchant. He owned a magnificent house with servants and carriages, beautiful clothes and jewels. Every meal the merchant had was a banquet to which only the wealthiest and most important people were invited.

To one of these banquets there came an old seer who could tell the future. And there, in front of all his guests, the seer told the merchant that one day all the merchant's wealth would be eaten by Yosef Mokir Shabbat! Everybody laughed because the idea seemed so ridiculous. But that night the merchant couldn't sleep. He was very fond of his wealth, and he thought of a plan to protect it.

Early the next morning, the merchant drove in his carriage to visit a friend in a distant town. The friend was happy to see him, and even happier at the offer the merchant made. "I will exchange all my property for your pearl," the merchant said. Now, this was no ordinary pearl; it was known to be priceless. The friend agreed, and the merchant drove away, relieved, knowing that he only had to hold on to the pearl, and his wealth would be safe.

It was a fine day, and the merchant took out the pearl to admire its beauty in the sunlight. Just then, as the carriage rattled over a wooden bridge, a strange wind blew up as if from nowhere and took the merchant by surprise. He reached up with his hand to hold his hat on, forgetting that his hand held the pearl. It dropped out of the carriage, through a crack in the bridge, and into the river below.

The next Friday, the market was thronged with people, and the stall owners were doing a great trade. Late in the afternoon, Yosef Mokir Shabbat appeared in the market. He just wanted one final look around, he wasn't sure why, perhaps to find something that would make the coming Shabbat perfect.

The fishmonger's wife saw him coming, and whispered to her husband, "Here comes your last chance! If anyone is foolish enough to buy this huge fish you've been trying to sell all day, that one will. You just have to..."
"I know what to do!" whispered the fishmonger.

"Yosef," he said, "I'd like to show you something – a fish fit only for Shabbat." Yosef looked at the big, beautiful fish. He knew he couldn't afford it, and his wife would shout at him if he bought it. He knew it was big enough to feed as many extra guests as he'd like to invite. He knew he'd have to sell his hat to buy such a fish. His heart was torn. Yosef Mokir Shabbat bought the fish.

That night, when all the shouting was over, and Yosef, his family and their guests were sitting at the dinner table eating the fish. Yosef cut himself a bite, and onto his plate dropped ... a pearl.

Vayikra is a book of laws. In this parasha, God tells Moshe about offerings that the Children of Israel must bring on special occasions if they want to give thanks or if they have done something wrong, even by accident. These offerings might be domestic animals or fruit or corn, and they are to be burned on the altar in the Mishkan by Aharon and the Kohanim. In those days, all peoples brought offerings or sacrifices; this was a natural form of worship. The Torah is different because the offering could be brought only after people had

repented for their sins, and paid for any damage they had caused. There was no "magic" involved: people admitted their guilt, were sorry, paid the price, and then "sacrificed" something that they owned so that they could feel closer to God.

28

1 *Plowing*
2 *Sowing*
3 *Reaping*
4 *Sheaf-making*
5 *Threshing*
6 *Winnowing*
7 *Selecting*
8 *Writing*
9 *Erasing*
10 *Separating into threads*
11 *Tying a knot*
12 *Untying a knot*
13 *Sewing*
14 *Tearing*
15 *Marking out*
16 *Building*

As we begin the book of laws, let's look at some of the laws connected to Shabbat. In the Ten Commandments, we read: Remember the Shabbat and keep it holy... you shall do no work. The Rabbis wanted to be sure they understood what God meant by *melacha,* work. They concluded that "work" would be defined as anything that had been done in order to build the Mishkan. They made a list of all forms of work included, and came up with 39, which are known as

avot melacha, categories of work prohibited on Shabbat. Later, the Rabbis interpreted these 39 categories so we could understand them in our lives. For example, "reaping" led the Rabbis to decide that we could not pick flowers on Shabbat.

Remember: the laws of Shabbat exist to make it holy and special, and to make us holy and special. Six days a week we master the world. On Shabbat, we are told to let the physical world rest, to be at harmony with creation. These laws help us to do that; they are laws that make us free.

THE 39 AVOT MELACHA

17 *Demolishing*	24 *Sheep-shearing*	31 *Slaughtering*	37 *Carrying in a public place*
18 *Kindling a fire*	25 *Bleaching*	32 *Skinning or flaying*	38 *Inserting thread into a loom*
19 *Extinguishing a fire*	26 *Combing raw material*	33 *Tanning*	39 *Removing the finished article*
20 *Sifting*	27 *Dyeing*	34 *Scraping*	
21 *Grinding*	28 *Spinning*	35 *The final hammer blow*	
22 *Kneading*	29 *Weaving*	36 *Cutting to shape*	
23 *Baking*	30 *Trapping*		

God instructed Moshe about what Aharon and the Kohanim must do when offerings were brought by the people. God described the rituals attached to all the different kinds of offerings. Then Moshe brought Aharon and his sons before all of the Children of Israel. He dressed them in their priestly clothing and anointed them so they could serve as Kohanim for the people, as God had commanded.

This Shabbat is also known as *Shabbat Hagadol,* the Great Shabbat, because it is the Shabbat before Pesach. We remember Pesach every Shabbat, because we say the phrase, *zecher leyitsiat mitsrayim,* a reminder of going out of Egypt, as part of the Friday night Kiddush. But on this Shabbat, there is an additional custom to read through the *Pesach Haggadah,* to prepare ourselves correctly for the *Seder.*

כשרות.

Kashrut:

A set of rules

which define

which foods

are permitted

for eating

Shabbat Shemini
שַׁבָּת שְׁמִינִי

God told Moshe and Aharon which animals, fish, birds and insects were *kosher*, permitted for the Children of Israel to eat, and which were not. In this way, God helped the people understand that they were holy and had a different way of life from other peoples. God also caused the Children of Israel to make eating something to think about, something to make people aware that they are on a different level from animals.

◄ EATING ON SHABBAT ►

Food and eating are always part of life. They are also a big part of Shabbat. In the part of the Talmud that deals with Shabbat, it is written: *What gives pleasure on Shabbat? Rav Yehuda, the son of Rav Shmuel, said in the name of Rav: a special dish cooked with spinach, large pieces of fish and cloves of garlic. Rav Hiya, the son of Ashai, said in the name of Rav: even something small, but made especially for Shabbat, would give pleasure.*

31

Shabbat Tazria-Metsora
שבת תזריע-מצורע

These two parshiot describe various things that can happen to the body, and how the Children of Israel were to treat them. One of the main things described is leprosy, a frightening and infectious disease that was common at that time. God told Aharon and his sons how to diagnose leprosy, and what to do to prevent an epidemic. The Torah touches on all aspects of the life of the people.

32

PREPARATIONS

If you have servants to do the work for you, do you still have the personal obligation to prepare for Shabbat? The Talmud says yes, you do, and it gives examples of famous scholars, and the things they would do with their own hands for Shabbat. Here are a few of them:

•*Rav Nachman would put the house*

in order, putting away weekday things and taking out the Shabbat things.

•*Rava would salt fish.*

•*Rav Huna would light the lights.*

•*Rav Papa would braid the wicks.*

•*Rav Hisdah would cut up beets.*

•*Rabbah and Rav Yosef would chop wood.*

•*Rav Zeira would light a fire.*

VAYIKRA

God told Moshe to say to the people: You shall be holy, for I, your God, am holy. God gave many examples of laws and prohibitions that would help the people become holy, special, set apart. One of them is: when you reap the harvest of your land, you shall not reap all the way to the edges of your field, or gather the gleanings of your harvest. You shall leave them for the poor and the stranger. These are laws of moral behavior, meant to create a nation worthy of God's words: I have set you apart from other peoples to be Mine.

MAKING SHABBAT SPECIAL

Shabbat is mentioned in this week's parasha, as an example of how God sets us apart. In the Midrash, we find this thought:

How do you mark Shabbat and make it special? With reading and discussing, with eating and drinking, with clean clothes and with rest.

How nice to have a law that we can have such fun fulfilling!

VAYIKRA

God gave Moshe particular laws for the Kohanim and their families, because they represented the people as they worked in the Mishkan. This parasha also presents the festivals and their laws: Rosh Hashana, Yom Kippur, Succot, Pesach, Shavuot and, of course, Shabbat.

SHABBAT QUEEN

הַחַמָּה מֵרֹאשׁ

הָאִילָנוֹת נִסְתַּלְּקָה

בֹּאוּ וְנֵצֵא

לִקְרַאת שַׁבָּת הַמַּלְכָּה

הִנֵּה הִיא יוֹרֶדֶת

הַקְּדוֹשָׁה הַבְּרוּכָה

וְעִמָּהּ מַלְאָכִים

צְבָא שָׁלוֹם וּמְנוּחָה

בֹּאִי בֹּאִי הַמַּלְכָּה

בֹּאִי בֹּאִי הַכַּלָּה

שָׁלוֹם עֲלֵיכֶם

מַלְאֲכֵי הַשָּׁלוֹם

Haim Nachman Bialik was considered the greatest modern Hebrew poet. He wrote a poem that became a well-loved song for Shabbat. In it, he continued the idea of Shabbat as a queen who comes to visit us once a week, accompanied by her "royal entourage" of angels. He also used the traditional song, Shalom Aleichem, as a framework. Here is the first verse of his poem:

The setting sun
is disappearing from the treetops
Come, let us go
and greet the Shabbat Queen
She is coming, holy and blessed
And with her
are angels of peace and of rest
Welcome, Queen!
Welcome, Bride!
Welcome to you, angels of peace!

Every seventh year God told Moshe, the land that I give you will have a Shabbat of its own. The Children of Israel will work the land for six years, but the seventh will be a year of rest for the land and for the people who worked it. That year would be called *Shmitah*. After seven Shmitah years, there would be an extra rest year, the fiftieth year, called *Yovel*.

During Shmitah, no crops would be planted and no vines would be pruned – the land would be at rest. During Yovel, slaves would be freed and land would return to its original owner. "The land is Mine," said God. "If you keep all of My laws and commandments, I will give you rains in their seasons, so that the earth shall yield its produce and the trees of the field their fruit. I will grant peace in the land."

RESTING

The laws of Shmitah and Yovel were good laws for the earth. Only now, when we have scientific research, do we realize that land must rest in order to produce better crops. In those days, other nations (the Romans, for instance) thought the Israelites were lazy for not working the land for a year. They also thought the Israelites were lazy for not working one day a week, on Shabbat! But now, the whole world knows that Shabbat is good for the earth – and good for the human soul, too.

במדבר

Moshe was told by God to count the men over twenty, in order to form an army. The people were counted by their tribes. Ya'akov's children had each produced many descendants, and the Children of Israel were divided into twelve tribes based on them, and called by their names. There was no tribe called Yosef, however. His two sons, Ephraim and Menashe, each had tribes named for them. The people camped and journeyed by tribe, and that is how they set off through the desert for the Promised Land.

The twelve tribes became a symbol of the whole nation. When God told Moshe how to make the special clothing for Aharon as the *Cohen Gadol*, the High Priest, God described an *ephod*, a breastplate, which would have twelve precious stones in it, to correspond to the twelve tribes.

Today we have forgotten the names of our tribes, unless we are Kohanim, priests, or Levi'im, both from the tribe of Levi. Instead, the Jewish people are divided into *Edot,* ethnic groups according to our countries of origin. We all have the same Torah, the same stories and laws, but over many years we have developed many different customs: the ways we dress, the melodies we use for songs, the food we eat, even the way we do certain rituals. We even developed several languages, besides Aramaic and Hebrew, which Jews everywhere use for study and prayer.

Sephardic Jews' ancestors lived in Spain, Morocco, Greece, Turkey and other countries in the Mediterranean area.

Ashkenazic Jews' ancestors lived in Germany, Russia, Poland and other European countries.

‎.ע ד ו ת.

Edot:

Jewish ethnic

groups according

to our countries

of origin, having

differing customs.

For example:

Sephardic Jews

spoke *Ladino,*

a language

based on Spanish

and Hebrew.

Ashkenazic Jews

spoke *Yiddish,*

a language

based on German

and Hebrew.

37

BAMIDBAR

The tribe of Levi was different from all the others. This tribe would camp and travel in the center of all the other tribes, to take care of the Mishkan. Within the tribe of Levi were the *Kohanim*, the descendants of Aharon, who took care of offerings to God, and had other special duties. The rest of the members of Levi helped them. The Kohanim in this parasha are given the words for the special blessing with which they were to bless the Children of Israel in God's name.

BLESSING OF THE KOHANIM

The blessing of the Kohanim, found in this parasha, is one we already know. It is also what parents say when they bless their children on Friday night. (The part that's for both boys and girls – *see Shabbat Vayechi.*) And every Shabbat morning, this blessing is said twice in the synagogue as part of the Shabbat prayers. The Kohanim or the *Chazan,* the person leading the prayers, stand up in front of the people and say this blessing over everyone present, just as they have been doing since the Children of Israel were in the desert!

Shabbat B'ha-alotcha
שבת בהעלותך

When the Children of Israel traveled in the desert, it was a major operation. There were hundreds of thousands of people, not to mention sheep and goats! They had two silver trumpets, which were blown to tell the people when it was time to travel. The *Aron,* the special box holding the stone tablets God gave Moshe on Mount Sinai, was carried in front of the people.

In spite of all the amazing things that had happened to them, the desert journey was a difficult transition for the former slaves. Some of them complained about their diet: "If only we had meat! We remember the fish we used to eat in Egypt, the cucumbers, the melons, the leeks, the onions and the garlic. Here, there's nothing but manna!"

וַיְהִי בִּנְסֹעַ

הָאָרֹן וַיֹּאמֶר מֹשֶׁה

קוּמָה יְיָ וְיָפֻצוּ אֹיְבֶיךָ

וְיָנֻסוּ מְשַׂנְאֶיךָ מִפָּנֶיךָ

ARON HAKODESH

Part of the Shabbat prayer service comes from this parasha. When we take the Torah out of the Aron today, we say:
When the Aron set out in front of the people, Moshe would say: Advance, God; May Your enemies be scattered before You.

When we return the Torah to the Aron, we say what Moshe said when the Aron was put to rest at the end of a journey in the desert:
Return, God, to the tens of thousands of the people of Israel

DELICACIES

מַה־יְּדִידוּת מְנוּחָתֵךְ, אַתְּ שַׁבָּת
הַמַּלְכָּה, בְּכֵן נָרוּץ לִקְרָאתֵךְ
∙∙∙∙∙∙∙
מֵעֶרֶב מַזְמִינִים כָּל מִינֵי מַטְעַמִּים,
מִבְּעוֹד יוֹם מוּכָנִים תַּרְנְגוֹלִים
מְפֻטָּמִים וְלַעֲרֹךְ כַּמָּה מִינִים,
שְׁתוֹת יֵינוֹת מְבֻשָּׂמִים, וְתַפְנוּקֵי
מַעֲדַנִּים בְּכָל שָׁלֹשׁ פְּעָמִים

On Shabbat, we don't have time to remember good meals of the past, because we're too busy eating! We are actually commanded to eat three festive meals every Shabbat, each accompanied by its own Zemirot, special songs sung only on Shabbat. At the first meal, on Friday night, we sing one that describes all the fabulous food we are meant to eat:

How beloved is your rest, Shabbat Queen. That's why we are in a hurry to greet you. From Shabbat evening all kinds of delicacies are in order: Plump chickens prepared during the day. Spiced wines of many kinds to drink. All kinds of special treats for all three meals.

Moshe sent twelve men, one from each tribe, to explore the Promised Land before the people entered it. They spent forty days there, and returned with a cluster of grapes so big, it took two people to carry it! But ten of the men said, "It is a land of milk and honey – but giants live there, and strong warriors in walled cities. We can't go there." Only Calev and Yehoshua said, "The land is beautiful and fertile. We can conquer it because God is with us."

But the people were afraid and said, "If only we had died in Egypt, or in this desert! Let's go back to Egypt." God became very angry. "I will do as you have said," God told them. "You will die in this desert. You will wander forty years, and your children will have the land when all of you are gone." The generation that came out of Egypt would not see the land.

NEWCOMERS

In a way, every group of immigrants is like the generation that came out of Egypt. They are afraid of what they will be expected to do in their new country. It is usually their children who really become a part of their new land. The newest immigrants to Israel are from the former Soviet Union. They are finding many things that are strange to them. One of these things is Shabbat.

Here is a letter written by a new immigrant to her relatives in Moscow, after arriving in Israel in 1990:

You know, Tanya, at first these Shabbats were very annoying. Imagine, for two days, you sit in your house like an idiot, you don't know where to put yourself.

And then one day a friend came over, and we decided to go for a walk. He promised to show me a pretty place. The place really was fantastic. I couldn't have imagined a place like it, a city within a city. We walked a long time through narrow streets lit by lights shining from windows. Then we heard singing coming from somewhere. We saw the corner of a table covered with a white cloth. There were candles. We saw well dressed people in white shirts, slowly singing and dancing. And you know, at that moment I was jealous to the point of tears, that we don't know something very important, we don't understand it, we don't feel it, and because of that we don't appreciate it. Something very important is happening right next to us, but we have no connection to it.

Shabbat Korach
שַׁבָּת קוֹרַח

Korach, of the tribe of Levi, and some men from the tribe of Reuven organized a rebellion of 250 men against Moshe and Aharon. "What makes you holier than we are?" they asked. "Why should you make yourself a prince over us?" The people began to listen to Korach and join his rebellion. Moshe said to the people, "Everything I have done has been what God asked me to do." Then God told Moshe: Tell the people to move away from the tents of Korach and his partners. Suddenly, the earth opened up. Korach and his followers were swallowed up by the ground. The rebellion was over. (Don't you wish life was like that today?)

ERUV

One of the things we are not permitted to do on Shabbat is to carry in a public place. This is a very difficult law. It means we cannot take things with us to synagogue, or to our friends' houses. The Rabbis thought about this law. They knew it was not meant to make Shabbat hard for us. They interpreted the meaning of "a public place" as any place that was not enclosed. So, if we put a fence around a yard, or a neighborhood, or even a whole city, then it is no longer a public place, and we can carry in it.

The Rabbis called this "fence", or enclosure, an Eruv. Today, many Jewish neighborhoods put up an Eruv to make it possible to carry on Shabbat. In Israel, almost every city has an Eruv around it. Some big cities in the diaspora such as Amsterdam and Seattle have Eruvs around their Jewish neighborhoods.

41

As the desert journey continued, the people complained that there was no water. God told Moshe to command a rock to give forth water. But when the time came, Moshe, with Aharon at his side, hit the rock with his stick instead of simply speaking to it. The people got their water, but God said to Moshe and Aharon: You did not believe in Me enough to make Me holy in front of the people. You will not bring them into the land.

The people traveled across many other lands on their journey. Moshe asked permission to cross these lands from their kings, but the kings always refused and attacked the Children of Israel on their way. Sometimes Israel beat them, but sometimes they were forced to choose a different way to travel. Aharon and Miriam, Moshe's brother and sister, died in the desert.

SHABBAT AFTERNOON

At the end of the 19th century, in the villages of Lithuania, there was a beautiful custom on Shabbat afternoons. All the young women of the village would go walking in the woods and sit under the trees in the middle of the forest. The young men would follow.

The young women would begin to sing Jewish folksongs. The young men, sitting apart, would join in. They would sing together, in harmony, under the sky, all afternoon. When it was time for the evening meal, they would walk slowly back to the village together.

42

Shabbat Balak
שבת בלק

Balak, the king of Moav, heard that Israel was coming, and he was afraid. He sent for Bil'am, a magician with powers of prophecy, to curse Israel for him. Bil'am set off on his donkey. God sent an angel to block his way. Bil'am couldn't see the angel, but the donkey could. The donkey tried to get around the angel, but she couldn't. She tried again. Finally, she just stopped in the middle of the road.

Bil'am was angry, and beat his donkey. God let the donkey speak. "What have I done to you, that you beat me?" asked the donkey. Bil'am suddenly saw the angel on the road, and said, "I will go back if God wishes." "No," said the angel, "Go, but you will say what God wants you to say." So Bil'am traveled to Moav. Each time he stood up to curse Israel, blessings came out of his mouth instead! Balak was furious and sent him home.

THE ROMANS THOUGHT...

The ancient Romans believed that the Jews fasted every Shabbat, because no smoke was seen coming from their houses that day.

43

Shabbat Pinchas
שבת פינחס

God told Moshe: The land will be divided among the tribes, with each family head receiving a share. Then the five daughters of Tselafchad, of the tribe of Menashe, came to talk to Moshe. They said, "Our father died in this desert and left no sons. We want his share of the land to belong to us." Moshe brought their case to God, and God said: Their request is just. So the law was set that land could be transferred to daughters as well as to sons.

OFFERINGS

וּבְיוֹם הַשַּׁבָּת שְׁנֵי כְבָשִׂים

בְּנֵי שָׁנָה תְמִימִם

וּשְׁנֵי עֶשְׂרֹנִים סֹלֶת

מִנְחָה בְלוּלָה בַשֶּׁמֶן וְנִסְכּוֹ

There is a plant that grows out of the stones of the Western Wall in the Old City of Jerusalem. This plant is very strong, and gets what it needs from the rock. It is called *tselef,* from the same root as *tselafchad* in Hebrew. The rabbis say this plant is like the daughters of Tselafchad. They also compare it to the Jewish people, because both can grow anywhere.

In this parasha, we read about the special offering brought in the Mishkan in honor of Shabbat. There was an offering brought every day, in order to bring the people closer to God, as was

the custom in those days in that part of the world. But for Shabbat, there was this extra offering as well.

Today, the passage decribing the Shabbat offering is part of the *Musaf* prayers for Shabbat, a special prayer service added on Shabbat, as a reminder of the extra Shabbat offering long ago:

On Shabbat, two yearling lambs without blemish, together with two-tenths of a measure of choice flour, with oil mixed in as a meal offering.

44

Shabbat Matot-Mas'ei
שַׁבָּת מַטּוֹת – מַסְעֵי

Israel fought a battle with Midian, at God's command, and won it. Members of the tribes of Reuven and Gad, who had a lot of cattle, saw that the land of Midian was good cattle country. They asked Moshe if they could receive their share of land in Midian, even though it was across the Jordan River from the land God had promised. Moshe said to them, "After all we have been through, are you sure you don't want to live with your people in our own land? And are your brothers to go to war while you stay here?" The two tribes pledged to help their people conquer the land of Canaan first, and Moshe promised them and half the tribe of Menashe the share of land they had requested.

And as the people stood on the plains of Moav near Jericho, across the Jordan from their Promised Land, God told them exactly how their land would be divided, according to the tribes of the Children of Israel.

דְּרוֹר יִקְרָא לְבֵן עִם בַּת

וְיִנְצָרְכֶם כְּמוֹ בָבַת

נְעִים שִׁמְכֶם וְלֹא יִשְׁבַּת

שְׁבוּ נוּחוּ בְּיוֹם שַׁבָּת

> ◄ **THE SECOND MEAL** ►

After going to synagogue on Shabbat morning or around lunchtime, it is time for the second meal of Shabbat. We say Kiddush, which we already know from the parshiot of Shabbat Ki Tisah and Shabbat Yitro. We have two loaves of challah, and we have another meal.

Afterwards, we sing more zemirot, the ones that belong to the second meal. After all the eating and singing, most people take a little nap, or rest – also part of Shabbat!

One of the songs for the second meal is called "Dror Yikra." It is a happy song, usually sung to a fast tune. The mood of the second meal is celebration.

God will proclaim freedom
For sons and daughters
And protect you
Like the apple of the eye
Your names will always be pleasant
Rest and relax on the day of Shabbat

45

דברים

The last book of the Torah is everything Moshe said to the Children of Israel before his death.

Sometimes he reminds them of things that happened, sometimes he explains things he did or he reveals additional laws to them. And in the end, Moshe is saying goodbye to his people.

On this Shabbat, Moshe reminds the people of the many places they have traveled, the battles they have fought and the fear that kept the generation of the desert from entering the land. "God was angry at me because of you," said Moshe. "I will not enter the Land."

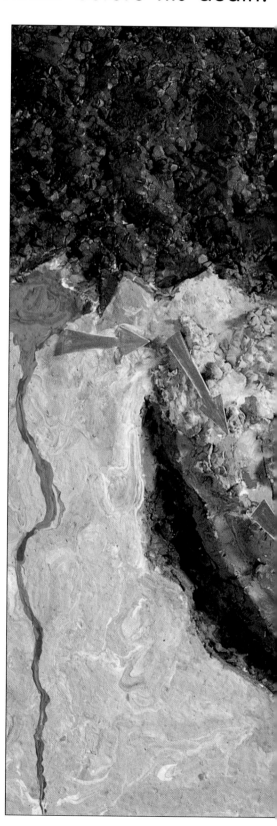

When we read this week's parasha, we really feel as if we were listening to Moshe ourselves "on the other side of the Jordan River, in the land of Moav." It

is as if he is speaking to each of us. That is the way we are always meant to listen to the Torah.

Every Shabbat, during *Shacharit,* the morning prayer, the Torah is taken out of the Aron in the synagogue. The Torah is carried around the synagogue, like Moshe carried the stone tablets down Mount Sinai. People touch the Torah as it passes. Someone reads the parasha of that Shabbat out loud, and all the people listen. Seven people are called up to the Torah while the parasha is read, to witness the reading and honor it. They say a *bracha,* a blessing:

Blessed are You, God,
Who chose us
from the other nations
and gave us the Torah.

The people are connected, by touching and hearing the Torah, to the story of their people and to God.

This Shabbat is also known as *Shabbat Hazon,* the Shabbat of the Vision. It is the Shabbat before *Tish'a B'av,* a day of mourning over the destruction of *Bet Hamikdash,* the Temple, and other disasters that have befallen the Jewish people. On this Shabbat, we read the prophet Isaiah's vision of Israel's destruction, to prepare us for the fast day to come.

Shabbat Va'etchanan/Nachamu
שבת ואתחנן/נחמו

Moshe reminded the people of what happened at Mount Sinai, when God spoke to them directly. "God did not make the covenant with your ancestors only; it was with every one of us here today. Your part is to keep God's laws. God's part is to give you the land promised to Avraham, Yitzchak, Ya'akov – and you. Teach this history, and this covenant, to your children."

KEEP AND REMEMBER

This Shabbat is also known as *Shabbat Nachamu*, the Shabbat of Comfort. It is the Shabbat after Tish'a B'av, and we are comforted after our mourning by reading Isaiah's vision of a better world to come. Isaiah comforted the Jews with this same vision after Bet Hamikdash was destroyed.

When Moshe repeats the words of the Ten Commandments in this parasha, he says, "Keep the Shabbat to make it holy." The first time we heard this commandment, on *Shabbat Yitro,* it was written as "Remember the Shabbat to keep it holy." The Midrash says the two words – Keep and Remember – were said by God at the same time, because both were equally important. One of the reasons we light two candles at the beginning of Shabbat is to remind us of these two aspects of Shabbat: to keep it, and to remember it.

Shabbat Ekev
שַׁבַּת עֵקֶב

Moshe told the people about the land they were about to receive. It is a good land, of wheat and barley, of grapevines, figs and pomegranates, of olives and dates. Living there will not be like living in Egypt. In their own land, their lives must be lived correctly, according to God's laws, so that God will bring the rain and help the crops grow. The people, the land and God are all related to each other.

שְׁמוֹר

אֶת

יוֹם

הַשַּׁבָּת

לְקַדְּשׁוֹ

JOY

The Torah knows that it will be easier for the people to keep God's laws if they are also blessed with a rich land, good food, and a comfortable life because of them.

Shabbat is a day full of laws, but also full of comfort and joy. In the Talmud, some of the Rabbis try to understand the meaning of Isaiah's saying: *You shall call Shabbat a joy.*

- Rabbi Abahu said, *Joy is lighting candles on Shabbat.*
- Rabbi Yirmiya said, *Joy means a visit to the bath house.*
- Rabbi Yochanan said, *Joy is washing your hands and feet in warm water.*
- Rabbi Yitzchak of Nafcha said, *Joy is a good deed.*

What do you think joy on Shabbat could mean?

49

Shabbat Re'eh
שַׁבַּת רְאֵה

Moshe said, "You will conquer your land from people very different from you, who worship gods of stone, on mountains and under trees. Do not be like them! You are holy. You are different."

Moshe also told them how to take care of each other, how to care for the poor and also the members of the tribe of Levi. Since the tribe of Levi, which included the Kohanim, had no land, and only worked to take care of the Mishkan and serve God, all the people had to donate one-tenth of their crops to Levi every year, so that they could live.

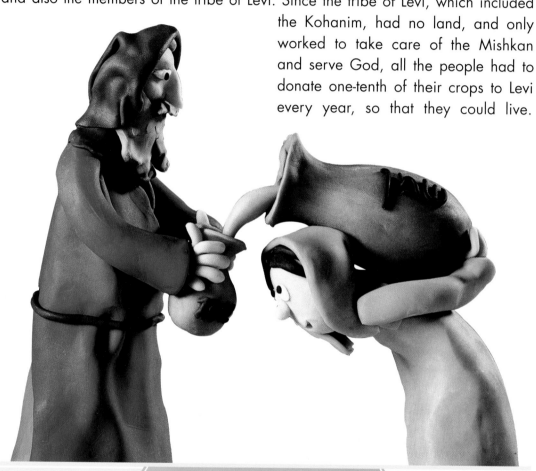

> **THE THIRD MEAL**

יְדִיד נֶפֶשׁ אָב הָרַחֲמָן

מְשׁוֹךְ עַבְדְּךָ אֶל רְצוֹנֶךָ

יָרוּץ עַבְדְּךָ כְּמוֹ אַיָּל

יִשְׁתַּחֲוֶה אֶל מוּל הֲדָרֶךָ

Right around sunset, or about an hour before Shabbat ends (or earlier, if Shabbat ends very late), it is time for *Seudah Shlishit,* the third meal. We are getting ready to say goodbye to Shabbat. There is no Kiddush. There is challah, but one is enough. There is usually not quite as much food, since we ate a major meal at lunchtime. And the mood is a little sad – after all, Shabbat with all its joy, is leaving us soon.

The songs for this meal are also a little sad and slow, to make us ready for the departure of the Shabbat Queen. One song traditionally sung at the third meal is *Yedid Nefesh.* It is a kind of love song to God.

Friend of my soul, Father of mercy
Bring Your servant to do Your will
Your servant will run like a hart
And bow down before Your glory
For Your love is more precious to me
Than the flavor of the best nectar

Shabbat Shoftim
שבת שופטים

D'VARIM

When you have problems among you, or are not sure you understand the laws, said Moshe, you will go to judges for decisions. They must be fair judges, who know the law and can decide for you. And if you should decide one day that you want a king over you, he must also be guided by the laws of the Torah.

When you go to war, here is who must *not* fight as a soldier: anyone who has built a new home, planted a new vineyard, become engaged to be married, or is simply afraid of battle. The nation must have rules, even at wartime, to protect itself and all its individual members.

MIZMOR LEDAVID

מִזְמוֹר לְדָוִד

יְיָ רוֹעִי לֹא אֶחְסָר

בִּנְאוֹת דֶּשֶׁא יַרְבִּיצֵנִי

עַל מֵי מְנֻחוֹת יְנַהֲלֵנִי

נַפְשִׁי יְשׁוֹבֵב

יַנְחֵנִי בְמַעְגְּלֵי צֶדֶק

לְמַעַן שְׁמוֹ

גַּם כִּי אֵלֵךְ בְּגֵיא צַלְמָוֶת

לֹא אִירָא רָע

כִּי אַתָּה עִמָּדִי...

אַךְ טוֹב וָחֶסֶד

יִרְדְּפוּנִי כָּל יְמֵי חַיָּי

וְשַׁבְתִּי בְּבֵית יְיָ

לְאֹרֶךְ יָמִים.

Another song for the end-of-Shabbat meal is *Mizmor LeDavid*, a psalm of King David. This, the 23rd psalm, is popular all over the world, for Christians and Jews.

God is my shepherd,
I have what I need.
God will let me lie down
in green pastures,
And lead me to quiet waters.
God renews my life

And guides me in
the right paths.
Even if I walk through
a valley of deepest darkness,
I am not afraid,
because You are with me.
Only goodness
and loving-kindness
will pursue me
All the days of my life,
And I shall live
in the house of God always.

51

Shabbat Ki Tetseh
שַׁבָּת כִּי תֵצֵא

D'VARIM

If you see your neighbor's lost sheep, or donkey, or cloak, you must return it, said Moshe. When you build a house, put a fence on the roof so no one will fall off. Be fair to those who work for you, Israelite or non-Israelite, and pay them on time. The laws of this parasha encourage people to care for each other's possessions and their feelings.

שִׁיר הַמַּעֲלוֹת

בְּשׁוּב יְיָ אֶת שִׁיבַת צִיּוֹן

הָיִינוּ כְּחֹלְמִים

אָז יִמָּלֵא שְׂחוֹק פִּינוּ

וּלְשׁוֹנֵנוּ רִנָּה

אָז יֹאמְרוּ בַגּוֹיִם

הִגְדִּיל יְיָ לַעֲשׂוֹת עִם אֵלֶּה

הִגְדִּיל יְיָ לַעֲשׂוֹת עִמָּנוּ

הָיִינוּ שְׂמֵחִים

CELEBRATION

Although many of our laws and customs are about relations between people, like the ones in this parasha, some of them are about relations with God. After every meal we eat, we must say a special prayer of thanks to God, called *Birkat Hamazon*, the Blessing of Food.

On Shabbat, before we begin Birkat Hamazon, we sing one of the psalms, in honor of the mood of joy that is ours on every Shabbat and holiday:

A song of ascending
When God brings back Zion
(we see it in a dream)
Our mouth will be filled with laughter
Our tongues with songs of joy
Then shall they say among the nations:
"God has done great things for them!"
God does great things for us,
and we shall rejoice.

52

D'VARIM

When you have settled in your land and are ready for your first harvest, said Moshe, take some of every first fruit of the soil, and bring it in a basket to the Kohanim. There you will remember your history, how you got to Egypt and how God freed you and gave you this land. You will leave your first fruits for God. In all that you do, remember what you promised God, and what God promised you.

BIRKAT HAMAZON

The bringing of first fruits was a way of thanking God for the land and for the food that grew on it. When we finish eating a meal, we must also thank God for the food we eat. Today, we say Birkat Hamazon instead of bringing a fruit offering. On Shabbat, we often sing part or all of this prayer together, to keep up the mood of celebration. Here is the first part of Birkat Hamazon:

Blessed are You, God,
Ruler of the universe,

who nourishes the whole world with
goodness, grace, kindness and mercy.
God gives food to all creatures
with everlasting kindness.
Through God's greatness,
we have never been in need;
may we never be in need,
for the sake of God's name.
For God nourishes everything,
and does good to all,
and provides food for all creatures.
Blessed are You, God,
Who feeds the world.

בָּרוּךְ אַתָּה יְיָ

אֱלֹהֵינוּ מֶלֶךְ הָעוֹלָם

הַזָּן אֶת הָעוֹלָם

כֻּלוֹ בְּטוּבוֹ

בְּחֵן וּבְחֶסֶד וּבְרַחֲמִים

הוּא נוֹתֵן לֶחֶם לְכָל בָּשָׂר

כִּי לְעוֹלָם חַסְדוֹ

וּבְטוּבוֹ הַגָּדוֹל

תָּמִיד לֹא חָסַר־לָנוּ

וְאַל יֶחְסַר לָנוּ

מָזוֹן לְעוֹלָם וָעֶד

בַּעֲבוּר שְׁמוֹ הַגָּדוֹל

כִּי הוּא אֵל זָן

וּמְפַרְנֵס לַכֹּל

וּמֵטִיב לַכֹּל וּמֵכִין מָזוֹן

לְכָל בְּרִיּוֹתָיו

אֲשֶׁר בָּרָא

בָּרוּךְ אַתָּה יְיָ הַזָּן אֶת הַכֹּל.

53

"This covenant is with everyone standing here and all those yet to be born," said Moshe. "The Torah is not beyond your reach. It is not in the heavens nor over the sea. It is very close to you, in your mouth and in your heart. I have put before you life and death; choose life, by loving God, living by God's Torah, in the land you will enter." Then Moshe called Joshua to him, and said: Be strong. You will lead the people in my place, and God will go before you.

בְּרִית.

Brit:

The covenant,

or agreement,

between

God and

the Children

of Israel.

ISAAC, THE BAKER

Sometimes the hardest thing to find is what is "very close to you." Sometimes, we do not know what treasures we possess... Once there was a baker, named Isaac, who lived in a small Jewish village. Everyone in the village bought their bread from Isaac, and he managed to make a living for his family. But there came a time of poverty, and people began to bake their own bread. Isaac got poorer and poorer, until one day he couldn't even afford to buy wood for his oven, and it became cold.

That night, Isaac had a dream. An old man with a long, white beard came to him and said, "Isaac! If you travel far from here, to the city of Prague, there, under the bridge in front of the King's palace, you will find a treasure!" The next night, the dream came back again, and the night after that as well. Isaac decided he couldn't ignore

a dream that returned three times, so he set off for Prague. It was a long journey, but Isaac finally arrived in the big city. He found the palace, and he found the bridge. He also found a guard, marching back and forth on the bridge. Isaac tried to look for the treasure, but the guard was always there. He was about to give up when, suddenly, the guard stopped marching and pointed at Isaac. "Who are you?" shouted the guard. "Are you a traitor, come to plot against the king? What's your business here?"

"I'm sorry, sir," said Isaac, "It was just a dream."

"Don't talk to me about dreams," said the guard. "For three nights, I have dreamed of an old man with a long white beard, who says, 'If you travel to a Jewish village, there, under the cold oven of a baker named Isaac, you'll find a treasure.' Who ever heard of a baker with a cold oven? And besides, all the Jews are named Isaac. Dreams mean nothing! Go home!"

So Isaac traveled back to his village, dug under his oven, and found a bag of gold! That night, Isaac had one more dream. The old man came to him and said: "Isaac! The treasure is finding what is already yours."

Shabbat Ha'azinu

שבת האזינו

Moshe recited a poem in praise of God, calling Heaven and Earth as witnesses to the story of the people of Israel. Then God said to Moshe, "Climb Mount Nevo, for there you are to die. You may see the land that I am giving to the people from a distance."

HAVDALLAH

It is hard for Moshe to say goodbye to his people, and he has taken the whole book of Devarim to do so. But now the moment of separation is almost here, and Moshe looks for words and actions that will make it special. Every week, when we say goodbye to Shabbat, we have a special ceremony called *Havdallah,* separation, to help us end Shabbat. The first part of Havdallah is a collection of lines from various parts of the Bible, like:

Once the Jews had light and joy,
gladness and honor.
May it be that way for us.
I lift up the cup of salvation,
and call on the name of God.

Then we say blessings over three things: a cup of wine, fragrant spices and a candle with two or more wicks. The wine is a symbol of joy and celebration. We begin Shabbat and end it with wine. The spices are a symbol of the sweetness and richness of Shabbat. We are sad that Shabbat is leaving, and the fragrant spices make us feel better. Creating a fire is our first act of creation for the new week. The two wicks bring together the "keep" and "remember" of the Friday night candles. We use all of our senses in Havdallah: we hear the words of the prayers, see and feel the candle flame, smell the spices and taste the wine. A new week begins. May we continue to use all our senses until the next Shabbat!

לַיְּהוּדִים הָיְתָה אוֹרָה

וְשִׂמְחָה וְשָׂשׂוֹן וִיקָר

כֵּן תִּהְיֶה לָּנוּ

כּוֹס יְשׁוּעוֹת אֶשָּׂא

וּבְשֵׁם יְיָ אֶקְרָא

55

D'VARIM

Moshe, the man of God, said goodbye to the people of Israel before he died. He spoke to each tribe by name, and gave them a blessing. Moshe climbed the mountain. God showed him the land, from north to south and from east to west, and said: "This is the land I promised to the Children of Avraham, Yitzchak and Ya'akov." Moshe died on the mountain, and Israel mourned him for thirty days. Joshua was filled with the spirit of wisdom, and became Israel's leader. But never again did there arise in Israel a prophet like Moshe.

Havdallah:

A special

ceremony

to help us

end Shabbat

56

SAYING GOODBYE

It was hard for Moshe and the people he led to be parted from each other. We are told that we have a *Neshama Y'teira*, an additional soul, that is part of us for Shabbat, and which leaves us at Havdallah. Moshe was the Neshama Y'teira of the people, and they would always remember.

Life is full of separations, and the last blessing of Havdallah is about separation: beween holy and secular, light and darkness, Israel and the other nations, Shabbat and the rest of the week. Then we sing a slow, sad song about Eliyahu the Prophet, who will bring the Messiah and redeem us one day. We let go of what is past, and dream of a better future, every single week. We look forward to next Friday when, once again the Shabbat Queen will arrive, and give us a taste of eternity.

זמירות שבת

Zemirot Shabbat

Here are some of the best known Shabbat Zemirot. The words are traditional, but each one has many melodies from all the countries and cultures in which Jewish people have lived. Now that you have learned about Shabbat, you are ready to celebrate it by singing the Zemirot.

עֶרֶב שַׁבָּת.

Friday night

These are

the first and last

verses of

Lechah Dodi,

which is sung in

synagogue

on Friday night.

Shalom Aleichem

is usually sung upon

returning home

from synagogue.

Lechah Dodi

Lechah dodi likrat kalah
P'nei Shabbat nekab'lah

Sh'mor vezachor bedibur echad
Hishmi'anu el ham'yuchad
Adonai echad u'shmo echad
Leshem uletiferet velit'hilah

Lechah dodi...

Bo'i veshalom ateret ba'alah
Gam besimchah uvetzahalah
Toch emunei am s'gulah
Bo'i chalah, bo'i chalah

Lechah dodi...

Shalom Aleichem

Shalom aleichem
Malachei hasharet
Malachei elyon
Mimelech malchei ham'lachim
Hakadosh baruch hoo

Bo'achem leshalom
Malachei hashalom
Malachei elyon
Mimelech...

Barchuni leshalom
Malachei hashalom
Malachei elyon
Mimelech...

Tzetchem leshalom
Malachei hashalom
Malachei elyon
Mimelech...

לְכָה דוֹדִי

לְכָה דוֹדִי לִקְרַאת כַּלָּה
פְּנֵי שַׁבָּת נְקַבְּלָה

שָׁמוֹר וְזָכוֹר בְּדִבּוּר אֶחָד
הִשְׁמִיעָנוּ אֵל הַמְיֻחָד
יְיָ אֶחָד וּשְׁמוֹ אֶחָד
לְשֵׁם וּלְתִפְאֶרֶת וְלִתְהִלָּה

לְכָה דוֹדִי...

בּוֹאִי בְשָׁלוֹם עֲטֶרֶת בַּעְלָהּ
גַּם בְּשִׂמְחָה וּבְצָהֳלָה
תּוֹךְ אֱמוּנֵי עַם סְגֻלָּה
בּוֹאִי כַלָּה בּוֹאִי כַלָּה

לְכָה דוֹדִי...

שָׁלוֹם עֲלֵיכֶם

שָׁלוֹם עֲלֵיכֶם
מַלְאֲכֵי הַשָּׁרֵת
מַלְאֲכֵי עֶלְיוֹן
מִמֶּלֶךְ מַלְכֵי הַמְּלָכִים
הַקָּדוֹשׁ בָּרוּךְ הוּא

בּוֹאֲכֶם לְשָׁלוֹם
מַלְאֲכֵי הַשָּׁלוֹם
מַלְאֲכֵי עֶלְיוֹן
מִמֶּלֶךְ...

בָּרְכוּנִי לְשָׁלוֹם
מַלְאֲכֵי הַשָּׁלוֹם
מַלְאֲכֵי עֶלְיוֹן
מִמֶּלֶךְ...

צֵאתְכֶם לְשָׁלוֹם
מַלְאֲכֵי הַשָּׁלוֹם
מַלְאֲכֵי עֶלְיוֹן
מִמֶּלֶךְ...

Tzur Mishelo

Tzur mishelo achalnu bar'chu emunai
Sava'anu vehotarnu kid'var adonai

Hazan et olamo, ro'einu avinu
Achalnu et lachmo, veyeyno shatinu
Al ken nodeh lishmo, unehal'lo befinu
Amarnu ve'aninu, ein kadosh kadonai

Tzur mishelo...

B'shir vekol todah nevarech eloheinu
Al eretz chemdah tovah
Shehinchil la'avoteinu
Mazon vetzeidah hisbi'a lenafsheinu
Chasdo gavar aleinu, ve'emet adonai

Tzur mishelo...

Yah Ribon

Yah ribon olam ve'olmaya
Ahnt hoo malka melech malchaya

Oved gvur'tech vetimhaya
Shfar kodmoch lehachavaya

Yah ribon...

Shvachin asader tsafra veramsha
Lach eloha kadisha
Di v'ra kol nafsha
Iyrin kadishin uv'nei enosha
Cheivat b'ra ve'ofei shemaya

Yah ribon...

צוּר מִשֶּׁלּוֹ

צוּר מִשֶּׁלּוֹ אָכַלְנוּ בָּרְכוּ אֱמוּנַי
שָׂבַעְנוּ וְהוֹתַרְנוּ כִּדְבַר יְיָ

הַזָּן אֶת עוֹלָמוֹ רוֹעֵנוּ אָבִינוּ
אָכַלְנוּ אֶת לַחְמוֹ וְיֵינוֹ שָׁתִינוּ
עַל כֵּן נוֹדֶה לִשְׁמוֹ וּנְהַלְלוֹ בְּפִינוּ
אָמַרְנוּ וְעָנִינוּ אֵין קָדוֹשׁ כַּיְיָ

צוּר מִשֶּׁלּוֹ...

בְּשִׁיר וְקוֹל תּוֹדָה נְבָרֵךְ לֵאלֹהֵינוּ
עַל אֶרֶץ חֶמְדָּה טוֹבָה
שֶׁהִנְחִיל לַאֲבוֹתֵינוּ
מָזוֹן וְצֵדָה הִשְׂבִּיעַ לְנַפְשֵׁנוּ
חַסְדּוֹ גָּבַר עָלֵינוּ וֶאֱמֶת יְיָ

צוּר מִשֶּׁלּוֹ...

יָהּ רִבּוֹן

יָהּ רִבּוֹן עָלַם וְעָלְמַיָּא
אַנְתְּ הוּא מַלְכָּא מֶלֶךְ מַלְכַיָּא

עוֹבַד גְּבוּרְתָּךְ וְתִמְהַיָּא
שְׁפַר קֳדָמָךְ לְהַחֲוַיָּא

יָהּ רִבּוֹן...

שְׁבָחִין אֲסַדֵּר צַפְרָא וְרַמְשָׁא
לָךְ אֱלָהָא קַדִּישָׁא
דִּי בְרָא כָּל נַפְשָׁא
עִירִין קַדִּישִׁין וּבְנֵי אֱנָשָׁא
חֵיוַת בָּרָא וְעוֹפֵי שְׁמַיָּא

יָהּ רִבּוֹן...

Friday night

We sing

these two songs

Friday night

at the Shabbat

dinner table.

עֶרֶב שַׁבָּת.

59

Shabbat day

We sing all

of these songs

at Shabbat

lunch.

Dunash Ben Labrat,

who wrote

Dror Yikra,

lived in Baghdad.

Yom Zeh Mechubad

Yom zeh mechubad mikol yamim
Ki vo shavat tzur olamim

Sheshet yamim ta'aseh m'lachtecha
Veyom hashvi'i l'elohecha
Shabbat lo ta'aseh vo m'lacha
Ki chol asah sheshet yamim

Yom zeh mechubad...

Rishon hoo l'mikraei kodesh
Yom shabbaton yom shabbat kodesh
Al ken kol ish beyeyno yekadesh
Al shtei lechem yivtz'u t'mimim

Yom zeh mechubad...

Dror Yikra

Dror Yikra leven im bat
Veyintzarchem kemo bavat
Na'im shimchem velo yooshbat
Shevu venoochu beyom Shabbat

Drosh navi ve'ulami
Ve'ot yesha asei imi
Nita sorek betoch karmi
She'ei shav'at b'nei ami

Droch purah betoch Botzrah
Vegam Bavel asher gavrah
Netotz tzarai be'af ve'evrah
Sh'ma koli beyom ekra

Elohim ten bamidbar har
Hadas shitah berosh tidhar
Velamazhir velanizhar
Shlomim ten kemei nahar...

יוֹם זֶה מְכֻבָּד
יוֹם זֶה מְכֻבָּד מִכָּל־יָמִים
כִּי בוֹ שָׁבַת צוּר עוֹלָמִים

שֵׁשֶׁת יָמִים תַּעֲשֶׂה מְלַאכְתֶּךָ
וְיוֹם הַשְּׁבִיעִי לֵאלֹהֶיךָ
שַׁבָּת לֹא תַעֲשֶׂה בוֹ מְלָאכָה
כִּי כֹל עָשָׂה שֵׁשֶׁת יָמִים

יוֹם זֶה מְכֻבָּד...

רִאשׁוֹן הוּא לְמִקְרָאֵי קֹדֶשׁ
יוֹם שַׁבָּתוֹן יוֹם שַׁבַּת קֹדֶשׁ
עַל כֵּן כָּל־אִישׁ בְּיֵינוֹ יְקַדֵּשׁ
עַל שְׁתֵּי לֶחֶם יִבְצְעוּ תְמִימִים

יוֹם זֶה מְכֻבָּד...

דְּרוֹר יִקְרָא
דְּרוֹר יִקְרָא לְבֵן עִם בַּת
וְיִנְצָרְכֶם כְּמוֹ בָבַת
נְעִים שִׁמְכֶם וְלֹא יֻשְׁבַּת
שְׁבוּ וְנוּחוּ בְּיוֹם שַׁבָּת

דְּרוֹשׁ נָוִי וְאוּלָמִי
וְאוֹת יֶשַׁע עֲשֵׂה עִמִּי
נְטַע שׂוֹרֵק בְּתוֹךְ כַּרְמִי
שְׁעֵה שַׁוְעַת בְּנֵי עַמִּי

דְּרוֹךְ פּוּרָה בְּתוֹךְ בָּצְרָה
וְגַם בָּבֶל אֲשֶׁר גָּבְרָה
נְתוֹץ צָרַי בְּאַף וְעֶבְרָה
שְׁמַע קוֹלִי בְּיוֹם אֶקְרָא

אֱלֹהִים תֵּן בַּמִּדְבָּר הַר
הֲדַס שִׁטָּה בְּרוֹשׁ תִּדְהָר
וְלַמַּזְהִיר וְלַנִּזְהָר
שְׁלוֹמִים תֵּן כְּמֵי נָהָר...

Shabbat day

Both these songs

were written

over 700 years ago.

Ki Eshmera Shabbat

was written by

Avraham Ibn Ezra

who lived in Spain.

Baruch El Elyon

was written by

Baruch Ben-Shmuel

who lived in

Mainz (now in

Germany.)

Ki Eshmera Shabbat

כִּי אֶשְׁמְרָה שַׁבָּת

Ki esh'mera Shabbat
El yishmereini

כִּי אֶשְׁמְרָה שַׁבָּת
אֵל יִשְׁמְרֵנִי

Ot hee le'olmei ad beino uveini

אוֹת הִיא לְעוֹלְמֵי עַד בֵּינוֹ וּבֵינִי

Asur metzo chefetz asot drachim
Gam miledaber bo divrei tzrachim
Divrei sechorah af divrei m'lachim
Ehegeh betorat El ut'chakmeini

אָסוּר מְצֹא חֵפֶץ עֲשׂוֹת דְּרָכִים
גַּם מִלְּדַבֵּר בּוֹ דִּבְרֵי צְרָכִים
דִּבְרֵי סְחוֹרָה אַף דִּבְרֵי מְלָכִים
אֶהְגֶּה בְּתוֹרַת אֵל וּתְחַכְּמֵנִי

Ot hee...

אוֹת הִיא...

Bo emtza tamid nofesh lenafshi
Hinei ledor rishon natan k'doshi mofet
Betet lechem mishneh bashishi
Kachah bechol shishi yachpil mezoni

בּוֹ אֶמְצָא תָמִיד נֹפֶשׁ לְנַפְשִׁי
הִנֵּה לְדוֹר רִאשׁוֹן נָתַן קְדוֹשִׁי מוֹפֵת
בְּתֵת לֶחֶם מִשְׁנֶה בַּשִּׁשִּׁי
כָּכָה בְּכָל־שִׁשִּׁי יַכְפִּיל מְזוֹנִי

Ot hee...

אוֹת הִיא...

Baruch El Elyon

בָּרוּךְ אֵל עֶלְיוֹן

Baruch el elyon asher natan menuchah
Lenafshenu pidyom mishet va'anachah
Vehoo yidrosh letziyon
Iyr hanidachah
Ad ana tugyon nefesh ne'enacha

בָּרוּךְ אֵל עֶלְיוֹן אֲשֶׁר נָתַן מְנוּחָה
לְנַפְשֵׁנוּ פִדְיוֹם מִשֵּׁאת וַאֲנָחָה
וְהוּא יִדְרוֹשׁ לְצִיּוֹן
עִיר הַנִּדָּחָה
עַד אָנָה תּוּגְיוֹן נֶפֶשׁ נֶאֱנָחָה

Hashomer Shabbat, haben im habat
La'el yeratzu, kemincha al machvat

הַשּׁוֹמֵר שַׁבָּת הַבֵּן עִם הַבַּת
לָאֵל יֵרָצוּ כְּמִנְחָה עַל מַחֲבַת

Rochev ba'aravot melech olamim
Et amo lishbot izen ban'imim
Bema'achalei areivot
Beminei mat'amim
Bemalbushei kavod
Zevach mishpachah

רוֹכֵב בָּעֲרָבוֹת מֶלֶךְ עוֹלָמִים
אֶת־עַמּוֹ לִשְׁבּוֹת אִזֵּן בַּנְעִימִים
בְּמַאֲכָלֵי עֲרֵבוֹת
בְּמִינֵי מַטְעַמִּים
בְּמַלְבּוּשֵׁי כָבוֹד
זֶבַח מִשְׁפָּחָה

Hashomer Shabbat...

הַשּׁוֹמֵר שַׁבָּת...

The third meal

These are

songs we sing

on Shabbat

afternoon.

Mizmor LeDavid

Mizmor leDavid
Adonai ro'i velo ech'sar
Bin'ot deshe yarbitzeini
Al mei menuchot yenahaleini
Nafshi yeshovev
Yancheini bema'aglei tzedek
Lema'an sh'mo
Gam ki eileich
B'gei tsalmavet lo iyra ra
Ki ata imadee

Shivt'cha umish'antecha
Heimah yenachamuni
Ta'aroch lefanai shulchan
Neged tsor'rai
Dishanta vashemen roshi
Kosi r'vaya
Ach tov vachesed yird'funi
Kol y'mei chayai
Veshavti beveit hashem
L'orech yamim

מִזְמוֹר לְדָוִד

מִזְמוֹר לְדָוִד
יְיָ רוֹעִי לֹא אֶחְסָר
בִּנְאוֹת דֶּשֶׁא יַרְבִּיצֵנִי
עַל מֵי מְנוּחוֹת יְנַהֲלֵנִי
נַפְשִׁי יְשׁוֹבֵב
יַנְחֵנִי בְמַעְגְּלֵי צֶדֶק
לְמַעַן שְׁמוֹ
גַּם כִּי אֵלֵךְ
בְּגֵיא צַלְמָוֶת לֹא אִירָא רָע
כִּי אַתָּה עִמָּדִי

שִׁבְטְךָ וּמִשְׁעַנְתֶּךָ
הֵמָּה יְנַחֲמֻנִי
תַּעֲרֹךְ לְפָנַי שֻׁלְחָן
נֶגֶד צֹרְרָי
דִּשַּׁנְתָּ בַשֶּׁמֶן רֹאשִׁי
כּוֹסִי רְוָיָה
אַךְ טוֹב וָחֶסֶד יִרְדְּפוּנִי
כָּל יְמֵי חַיָּי
וְשַׁבְתִּי בְּבֵית יְיָ
לְאֹרֶךְ יָמִים

Yedid Nefesh

Yedid nefesh av harachaman
M'shoch avd'cha el r'tzonecha
Yarutz avd'cha k'mo ayal
Yishtachave el mool haderech
Ye'erav lo yedidotecha
Minofet tzoof v'chol ta'am

Hadoor na'eh ziv ha'olam
Nafshi cholat ahavatecha
Ana el na r'fa na lah
Beharot lah no'am zivecha
Az titchazek vetitrapei
Vehaytah lah simchat olam

Vatik yehemu na rachamecha
Vechusa na al ben ahuvecha
Ki zeh kamah nichsof nichsafti
Lirot betiferet uzecha
Eleh chamdah libi
Vechusa na v'al titalem

Higale na uf'ros chavivi alai
Et sucat shlomecha
Ta'ir eretz mi'kvodecha
Nagilah venism'chah bach
Maher ehov ki va mo'ed
Vechaneinu ki'ymei olam

יְדִיד נֶפֶשׁ

יְדִיד נֶפֶשׁ אָב הָרַחֲמָן
מְשׁוֹךְ עַבְדְּךָ אֶל רְצוֹנֶךָ
יָרוּץ עַבְדְּךָ כְּמוֹ אַיָּל
יִשְׁתַּחֲוֶה אֶל מוּל הֲדָרֶךָ
יֶעֱרַב לוֹ יְדִידוֹתֶיךָ
מִנֹּפֶת צוּף וְכָל טָעַם

הָדוּר נָאֶה זִיו הָעוֹלָם
נַפְשִׁי חוֹלַת אַהֲבָתֶךָ
אָנָּא אֵל נָא רְפָא נָא לָהּ
בְּהַרְאוֹת לָהּ נֹעַם זִיוֶךָ
אָז תִּתְחַזֵּק וְתִתְרַפֵּא.
וְהָיְתָה לָהּ שִׂמְחַת עוֹלָם

וָתִיק יֶהֱמוּ נָא רַחֲמֶיךָ
וְחוּסָה נָא עַל בֵּן אֲהוּבֶךָ
כִּי זֶה כַּמָּה נִכְסֹף נִכְסַפְתִּי
לִרְאוֹת בְּתִפְאֶרֶת עֻזֶּךָ
אֵלֶּה חָמְדָה לִבִּי
וְחוּסָה נָא וְאַל תִּתְעַלָּם

הִגָּלֵה נָא וּפְרֹס חֲבִיבִי עָלַי
אֶת סֻכַּת שְׁלוֹמֶךָ
תָּאִיר אֶרֶץ מִכְּבוֹדֶךָ
נָגִילָה וְנִשְׂמְחָה בָּךְ
מַהֵר אֱהֹב כִּי בָא מוֹעֵד
וְחָנֵּנוּ כִּימֵי עוֹלָם

.סְעוּדָה שְׁלִישִׁית

The third meal

Together

the first letters

of each verse

spell the name

of God.

63

The
Shabbat Book

*Also available from
the Scopus Shabbat series*

The Shabbat Activity Book

Shalom Shabbat Video
Song and stories with
Chaim Topol, Hanny Nachmias
and clay animation

Shalom Shabbat
Audiocassette with Shabbat songs
to sing with the whole family

Other products from Scopus

The Animated Haggadah
Book, video & activity book

The Animated Menorah
Book & activity book

Megillat Esther
Illustrated scroll & activity book

Shirim K'tanim
Series of eight videos
and book of Hebrew songs
for children

Fliegel's Flight
A video bird's-eye view
of Jewish history